THE
THINGS
THAT
ARE
STUCK
IN
MY
HEAD..

LETTER FROM THE AUTHOR:

This is a collection of thoughts that I normally keep to
myself.
I decided to write the stuff that wonders in my head.
I'm excited to share this with you,
Use this book to escape your reality.

Yours truly,
Manny Flores

FoReWoRd:

Thank you for opening this book and giving me a chance, I promise you won't regret it. While you read this book, you should read it with an open mind. Some of these poems are very random--they are meant for you to think about life. Some of the poems are about me, and situations I have faced, and some of them are completely fictional. These scattered thoughts keep me up at night, sometimes they won't let me sleep. When I was younger I use to think I was weird because all these things were in my head, and maybe I am weird and I just haven't came to terms with it yet. Some of these poems are very dark, but that's where my mind leads me sometimes. I want to dedicate this book to my friends Ben and Focus: Thank you for always believing me, you are my brothers for life. I understand that life won't always be perfect and it doesn't have to be. Most of my best work has come from times where I was down and out.

To Maria Martin: Thank you.

IT BEGINS...

FIRES

THE FIRE IN MY HEAD WON'T STOP BURNING.
I WAKE UP TURN MY ALARM OFF,
GO ON WITH MY DAY
WHEN PEOPLE ASK HOW I AM DOING I SAY, "I AM FINE"
I KNOW THE FIRES WILL GO AWAY SOMEDAY
HOPEFULLY SOMEDAY SOON..

-MF

LOVE

WHAT IS LOVE ?
HOW DO YOU KNOW YOU ARE IN LOVE ?
IS LOVE TEMPORARY ?
IS LOVE PERMANENT ?
CAN YOU LIVE WITHOUT THE PERSON YOU LOVE?
CAN THE PERSON YOU LOVE BE MULTIPLE PEOPLE?
CAN YOU HATE THE PERSON YOU LOVE?
CAN YOU LOVE THE PERSON YOU HATE?
LOVE IS WHAT?

-MF

LONELY

BEING LONELY SUCK, ESPECIALLY IF YOU ARE CONSTANTLY AROUND OTHER
PEOPLE.
PEOPLE SAY, "BUT YOU'RE IN GRAD SCHOOL,
IM SURE YOU HAVE YOUR LIFE TOGETHER".
IF IT WAS ONLY THAT SIMPLE..
WHAT DOES MY DAD THINK?
DOES HE GET LONELY ALSO?
I GUESS I'LL NEVER KNOW.

-MF

Lebron James

How did lebron feel knowing he was great?
Did he ever question his ability?
Does he still doubt himself?
Does he ever get scared still ?
Does he think he isn't good enough?
What is it like to be king james?

-MF

Mother

I wish you could show me love.
I'm 24 but i still feel like i'm an 8 year old looking for his dad.
I know you are tired from work, and i respect it.
Sometimes i wish i could hear you say that you are proud of me.
I know that you are,
I just want to hear it.
That makes me feel better when i hear it.
I work so hard to make you happy,
Are you happy?
I don't know
What is happiness anyway?

-MF

Trippy vibes

It's the 70's all over again, and everyone is on acid.
I can feel your love
Or is that the acid talking?
Nah, i know you love me.
You told me so before we started rolling,
You also said you'll be here forever.
That makes me feel good.
I can see myself with you too.
Forever.

-MF

Undocumented dreamer

We're undocumented, but does that make a difference?
I don't think so.
We'll continue achieving, and breaking down barriers.
Go ahead and build that wall,
we'll just learn to fly next.
Undocumented and unafraid,
That is beautiful.
Dear undocumented dreamer,
What do you think about at night?
I would love to hear it.

-MF

Loaded pistol

The pistol sits on the dresser next to the coke.
She already lined up two for me.
My hand keeps shaking,
I don't know if it's the adrenaline or the drugs I have taken.
Either way, I can't go back now.
I hate committing crimes but how else will I feed my daughter?
The lord will understand.
I honestly hope he does.
But even if he doesn't..

It's Time.
(door shuts)

-MF

VICE CITY

"Big money, Big Booty Bitches,
That's going to be the death of me"
Dam, thats a great line.
Shoutout K.dot

-MF

Abandonment issues

Why did you leave us?
I know You and mom had issues, but you didn't have to abandon us.
I never tell anyone this, but I think about it sometimes.
I wish we got to play catch together.
I wish you could of put me on your shoulders at disneyland.
I wish you were there when i was getting locked up.
I needed you.
Moms needed you.
But we made it
Without you.

-MF

No Father Figures

No father figures,
Just a bunch of rappers that raised us.
Biggie, Tupac, Mac Dre
I'll Let you Chose.
One thing I do know is,
the bitch better have my money.
pardon my ignorance,
That's the music talking.
I can talk about music all day.

-MF

Absent Father

Hello Son,
Where can i start.
I never meant to abandon you,
It's just me and your mom weren't working out.
I know you feel like i gave up on you
But i didn't.
I would like to have a fresh start with you.
What do you say ?
Wanna grab coffee.

-MF

Loud Noises

I could never fall asleep,
It's almost 3am now.
Hearing my mom cry sucks.
I overheard her say, we might get kicked out.
The rent is due.
She told me nothing will happen to us,
But I know she is lying.
I know things won't be alright.
But I turned around and hugged her
And told her, "you are right".

-MF

LIES

"Why do you have to lie"?
Don't you know that i love you?
You said last time would be the last time.
It hurts me everytime i catch you cheating on me.
I thought about killing myself.
But i can't live without you.
Can you promise me that you will stop hurting me?
Please.
I don't know what i would do without you.
Just hold me babe,
And Don't let go.

-MF

JDA

"You don't have what it takes,
You are not ready for doctoral studies."
That's what my professor told me.
If you are so smart, why can't you see that i'm going to make it?
Stupid fool.
Do you need to add any more fire to the fuel?
As if i needed more.
You will see tho.
I'm going to make you eat those words.
Stupid fool.
Idols become your rivals
I thought that was just in music.
But Why am i competing if i already won?
Stupid fool.

-MF

CRAZY PILLS

I'm going crazy again.
How can people not see my vision?
Seeing is believing,
So i'm going to turn all of you, into believers.
All eyes on me.
Don't stop looking now,
Or you might miss this.
I've been practicing my touchdown celebrations.
I'll see you in the endzone.

-MF

Boondocks

Am I Huey?
Am I Riley?
Am I both?
How can I tell?
Please send a sign.
I'm drowning.
Send help.

-MF

Life is not what it seems

I'm coming.
Please be warned,
I think you can.
Can you feel it?
I feel it coming
I think about it so much it hurts.
I stay up late and think.
That's what I want to be.
The greatest,
(read backwards)

-MF

Blank soul

Dear Blank soul,
You are neither good nor evil
Thank you.

-MF

Boundless Potential

When I see you,
I see your potential.
What do you see, when you look at yourself?
Is it glory?
Is it demise?
Do you feel proud?
Or do you feel empty?
I wish you could see,
What I see .
I see a lion.
I see an animal.
I see greatness.
But you don't see it.
Waste of boundless potential.

-MF

DRUGS

(ALLIE'S VOICE 1993)

I NEED TO SMOKE, DO YOU HAVE BACKWOODS?
I HAD A VERY HARD DAY.
I BROUGHT OVER SOME 40OZ IF YOU WANNA DRINK WITH ME.
I LOVE IT WHEN YOU GET FUCKED UP WITH ME.
DO YOU STILL HAVE THAT COCAINE PLUG?
YOU SHOULD CALL HIM.
I WANT A GRAM.
I DON'T WANT TO ESCAPE REALITY,
I JUST LOVE THE WORLD THAT WE SHARE.
THE XANNIES WE TRIED YESTERDAY WERE GREAT.
YOU FUCKED THE SHIT OUT OF ME TOO.
PEOPLE CAN CALL US DRUG ADDICTS
BUT THEY DON'T UNDERSTAND.
OUR PARENTS NEVER LOVED US,
BUT WE LOVE EACH OTHER.
AND THAT'S WHAT MATTERS.

-MF

Pain

The Pain sucks,
But This shit will go away soon.
I don't wanna feel anymore.
I don't wanna see anymore.
I don't wanna be alive anymore.
Please.
I
Just
Want
The
Pain
To
Go
Away.

-MF

Happiness

I love talking to you.
When you talk I always listen.
As long as I'm alive,
You will have someone to hold you.
Someone to love you.
And someone to always make you feel appreciated.
I appreciate you.
I love you.
I enjoy being with you.
I have experienced many emotions,
And by far, loving you is the best one.
I love you
I love you
I love you

-MF

Writer's Block

I love writing.
It helps me escape my dark reality.
When i write, i make the rules.
I can write about untold riches.
I can write about being happy.
Otherwise, that stuff isn't likely.
Writing helps me see the truth for what it is
Writing helps me make up my own truth
Writing is
Powerful
Writing is
Life
Writing is
Everything.

-MF

Soulmate

Where are you.
I need you right about now
I needed you a year ago
I take that back.
I needed you 10 years ago
Please show up.
I bet life would be so much fun with you.
Please take care.
Until then,
My beautiful soulmate.

-MF

MARIA MARTIN PT. 2

MARIA.
MIA.
MANNY.
THAT'S HOW PERFECT IT WAS SUPPOSED TO BE
WE HAD LIFE PLANNED OUT.
AND NONE OF THOSE PLANS CAME TRUE.
I'M THE ONE TO BLAME FOR THAT,
I TAKE FULL RESPONSIBILITY.
I LOVE YOU AND I ALWAYS WILL,
MARIA MARTIN.

-MF

SOCIETY

I hate society.
Making me feel bad for not being normal.
Who wants to be normal anyway?
Normal people are basic.
<u>I'm not basic.</u>
But why must i hide my stench of weed before i leave the house.
Would you not accept me?
I want to show you who i really am
But i'm self-conscious.
Will my tattoos scare you?
Or will that make you want to know my story.
I bet you'll like me if you got to know me.
But you will judge me before then.
Oh society.

-MF

Born A star

To Ben Astrolabio, With Love

You were Born a Star,
So why do you refuse to shine?
Just because people can't see that you are a star,
Doesn't mean you aren't a star.
Being a star is hard,
You have to do star shit.
If you try to settle for less,
You will never feel complete.
You were born a star,
So go out there and shine.

-MF

Classroom Magic

Poof!

So the boy appeared.

Everyone is wondering,

Where did he come from?

I wish i had an answer.

I'm just as confused as you.

But while i'm here,

Let me get a pencil.

-MF

Friends in need

TO my homie focus.

Big chillin after school, playground shit.
That is legendary.
To live and to travel is everything.
Let's take over the world so we can live forever.
I think i got the last round, so you owe me.
Henny and coke.
The usual.

..

93' til forever.

-MF

Money

MONEY IS THE ROOT OF ALL EVIL.
THAT'S ALL I'M SEEING LATELY.
DO I CHASE MONEY OR HAPPINESS?
HOW MUCH IS ENOUGH MONEY?
HOW MUCH IS ENOUGH HAPPINESS?
DECISIONS DECISIONS.
I DON'T HAVE MUCH TIME,
I HAVE TO MAKE A DECISION.

-MF

Does Everything have to be so dark?

"You can write positive content
Right"?

Uhhhhh yea i think so.

The birds fly high
And the
The sky is blue.
See! i'm not so bad.
Who am i kidding.

Just fake a smile and move on.

-MF

Best Wishes

If I had a wish, I would wish it all away.
I would wish for a fresh start,
I would wish that the sun stayed out all day.
I would wish my dreams come true.
I would wish for a million things.
I would wish for happiness.
I really would.
I would wish us back together.
What would you wish for?

-MF

Best rapper alive

This poem is dedicated to Hector Woods, With love

You are the underground king.
You are the best rapper around.
You just haven't written any raps yet.
The world is your canvas ,
All your missing is your paintbrush.
The day you find it, will be the day you find yourself.
Let your mind wonder
It's okay to be free.
We must allow ourselves to feel
I can't wait til the day you realize your hidden power.
The world is ready to be painted,
You just need your paintbrush.

-MF

Bart Tunes

The lonely rider sits,
wondering about the world.
Different people come on,
Different people get off.
But the lonely rider just sits there
Thinking, Wondering about the world.
He has a million questions.
But zero answers.
The lonely rider sits there
Wondering,
Thinking about the world.
..

"San leandro, next stop"
I grab my bag, my exit is next.

-MF

WRITER

I'M NOT A WRITER.
I'M NOT A POET.
I'M NOT AN AUTHOR.
I'M NOT ANYTHING.
I AM MANNY.
I AM DAMAGED.
I AM FIGHTING BACK.
I AM FREEING MYSELF.
I AM LIBERATED .
I AM WHATEVER YOU WANT ME TO BE.
BUT , I JUST WANT TO BE MYSELF.

-MF

Creative Freedom

Does my ex still think about me?
Does she still miss me
I wonder if i cross her mind from time to time.
I wonder is she feels better now
That she doesn't have to deal with an "ain't shit nigga"
Those were her last words to me.
Who am i kidding.
She is gone.
Just like everyone else.

-MF

Under so much stress

Damn me for being so stressed
Damn me for feeling so normal when there is complete chaos
Damn stress for getting the best of me.
Damn me for making my best work under stress
Damn life for not preparing me .
Damn.
What's going to happen when the stress goes away
Will i be the same person
Or will i change?
Only one way to see
damn.

-MF

Instagirl

Hello Instagram girl
Living the instagram world.
Valuing likes over real love.
Why do you let strangers determine if you beautiful or not?
I think you're perfect.
Less social media and more social connection.
That sounds perfect.
So what do you say ?
Let's go on a date?
Or should i just hit up your DM.

-MF

I'm not manny

My name is not manny
I don't know who i am.
I don't know what i've become.
I don't recognize myself anymore.
I'm not the person i once was.
What am i now?
What have i become?
I'm scared

-MF

No title

I apologize for being so dark,
I can't help it.
Everything has been without light for a while now.
I wonder if anybody can see it?
I get this feeling like things are ending.
Nothing is ever constant anyway.
I'm sorry if you don't recognize me anymore.
I barely recognize myself.
I'm sorry if you think i forgot.
I'm sorry,
I truly am.

-MF

Classroom thoughts

I'm in class but my mind won't stop wondering off
All I can think about is my mother
Will I graduate in time to pay for her surgery
That's the only reason why i'm in school
I hope she makes it
I know she will.

-MF

I

Love and Hate

Can you love and hate yourself at the same time?
I hate what i was
But i love what i'm becoming.
I sometimes feel worthy
I sometimes feel worthless.
I have a masters degree
It can't be all that bad, right?
I wish.
All have all these thoughts in my head
Hopefully writing them down will make them go away
I love and hate myself

-MF

Sexting

When do you get off work?
I think we should sext later.

-MF

Rainey Peak

In 9th grade you were wild.
By the way you are a liar lol.
You told me a million stories.
Half of them were made up.
you were you so smart,
Yet so crazy.

-MF

Love part 2.

Just love
That's it
Don't spread hate.
Life is easier when you're loving.
If you don't believe me,
Try it for yourself.
And watch the quality of your life change.

-MF

Manifest

At what point can i start gloating?
Or should i remain humble.
I don't know how to mix the two.
You see
I came along way
And i have a long way to go.
I guess i should just put my head down and go.
When do i get a break then?
Maybe in a few years.

-MF

If you're reading this. .

First of all thank you.
I really mean that.
For me to share this with you took a lot.
I'm uncomfortable sharing my thoughts to people
I must admit this was really healing.
You are watching me grow.
Thats beautiful.
I remember being lost at 17.
Not that i found myself yet,
because i truly feel that i haven't.
But i'm on the way.
Im grateful for everything.
Once again,
Thank you.

-MF

Dear future son,

We Made it!
Just wait till you are born.
I've been working really hard.
You will have the stuff I never had.
You will have a dad.
We are going to play catch together.
I'll take you to disneyland.
And I promise to be there for all of your graduations.
You will need me.
And I will need you.
We will make it.
Together.

-MF

DRUG INDUCED POETRY.

"After this one I'll stop"
That's what I always tell myself.
But who am I kidding,
I will never change.
Why am I like this?
I wish I would've never tried it.
I wish I stayed in school and did better.
Life can't get any darker.
I might as well take another hit.
After that one, i'll stop.

-MF

Accomplishments

I can't wait
Tomorrow is the big day.
Im finally graduating.
After 6 years of this PHD program
This is everything i ever wanted.
This is everything i worked for .
I don't even know how to feel.
I cant believe im actually happy.

-MF

Maried Girl

I can't believe you went and got married.
I thought i was supposed to be the one.
I feel like you punched me.
Is there any way we can make it work?
I cant believe im saying this,
but
But i can't wait for your divorce.
I'll be here.
waiting.

-MF

Fool me twice.

Shame on me.
Shame on me for believing you.
Shame on me for giving you a second chance.
Shame on me for thinking things would be different.
Shame on me for wanting to be happy with you.
Shame on me for being so stupid
Shame on me for believing in us.

-MF

CRAZY WORLD

Crazy life,
Crazy world,
Why am i so lost?
Crazy life ,
Crazy world,
Why am i so lost?
Crazy life,
Crazy world,
Why am i so lost?

-MF

Tattoo

I got my first tatt in santa barbara
And It was just what i wanted.
My appreciation for it eventually faded,
And I ended up getting it removed.
Shit happens.

-MF

CREATIVE GENIUS

California's Kanye West
The bay area's Jay Z
San Leandro's E-40
Cascades' John Lennon
Imitation is suicide
So I'll just be myself.
Thank you.

-MF

Married couple

I want to run away and get married
What do you say?
Let's go half on a baby?
And a dog?
I can make breakfast
And go on walks at the beach.
Everything can be perfect.
It's just the way i imagine it.

-MF

7am in new Orleans

It's 7am and we haven't been to sleep yet,
It's my first night here so it's only right.
The drip is coming down,
This corona is helping tho.
The food should be delicious.
Maybe i'll find my soulmate in this beautiful city.
Maybe i should go to sleep.
It's 7am in new orleans.

-MF

Kimberly

To my beautiful friend kim

When i hear that name i smile.
Who is kimberley?
Kim, is someone who always smiles.
And i like that.
No matter how hard life is,
She smiles.
Oh kimberley.
Thank you.
Never stop smiling.
Because The day you stop,
Will be the day you stop being you.

-MF

9pm in Manhattan

It's 9 Pm and it's time to catch my greyhound again
Back to philadelphia i go.
I like traveling,
But i'm alone.
That's the only thing that remains the same.
Being alone.
New city,
New friends,
Same loneliness.
It's not as bad anymore tho.
I don't cry like i used to.
I'll go to boston soon,
But i'll still be alone.

-MF

2PM IN MIAMI

Hella girls trying to be something their not.
Hella dudes trying to be something their not.
I'm trying to be something I'm not,
-successful.
You see that's all I want in life.
I also want a lamborghini
I think I'll have it soon.
South beach is beautiful.
It's 2 pm and I'm drunk.
That's how life should be

-MF.

6969

Me under you,
You under me.
That's when life is at its best.
69 is my favorite position
To give and get,
That's what life's all about.
I'll continue giving.
We all have a gift.
And that is to love.

-MF

RENDEZVOUS

We should fall in love together.
Meet me at the rendezvous.
I'll be there at 7pm.

-MF

Mirror

When you see me,
What do you see?
Do you see my scars
Or do you see my potential
If you can you past my bruises
You can see the real beauty.
For i can make you happy.
You are what you attract, i'm very attracted to you.
It's like looking at a mirror
We're very similar.

-MF

Page 72

65 poems later,
and I still don't have the right words to get you back.
What do I say?
Is there anything I can even say?
I've hurt you deeply.
I don't think we can recover from this.
Page 72,
The page I realized the truth:
That You aren't coming back.
I wish you the best.

-MF

Gym Girl

To the girl at 24 hour fitness,
I think your name is jessica.

I love staring from a distance
You are recreating your temple.
I love that about you.
The way your booty flexes when you're coming up from your squats.
I think i'm in love.
But I won't bother you,
I'll just keep staring at perfection.
Beautiful gym girl.

-MF

Next move

Now what?
She's gone.
What do I do now?
I don't even know if I can love somebody else.
I need time to heal
I need time to get better
I must pick up a million pieces from the ground
Someone will help me put them together
-MF

"MANNY YOU'RE PERFECT"

I'M NOT PERFECT STOP SAYING THAT.
I DRINK.
I SMOKE.
I CURSE.
I CUT PEOPLE OFF WHEN I'M DRIVING.
I STILL LICK MY FINGER AND PUT IT IN PEOPLES EAR.
I CHEATED ON THE PERSON WHO LOVED ME.
I TALK SHIT ,
I GET JEALOUS.
I'M NOT PERFECT.

-MF

Stupid Bitch

The Stupid bitch left,
Im lowkey mad
Not because she left,
But because she took my hoodie.
It was polo!
Maybe she can give it to her new dude.
He can have my hoodie.
Still won't be me,
Stupid bitch.

-MF

Boyfriend

It sucks you got a boyfriend
Does he even compliment you daily?
How many times has he told you he appreciates you today?
You see girl,
I can show you the stars and the moon from my spaceship.
What do you say?
Want to go out for a ride?
Just two innocent souls
Wandering space.
Don't worry about him
You won't miss out on anything
Come on Let's go.

-MF

Family Failure

I'm the failure of the family
Everyone graduated college except for me.
Why can I be perfect?
It seems like they are all happy.
I wonder what that feels like.
I guess i'll never know.

-MF

Wonderland

We popped a pill, now we're in a different planet.
I'm not scared.
We like it here.
This is when we come, when we want to be happy.
So tell me,
What brings you here?
I'm sure there's something you're escaping from.
So what is it?
We don't judge here.

-MF

Cant stop, WOnt stop.

More Attempts at being number one,
More Failures.

I can't stop tho.

More Sleepless nights.
More tears.

I can't stop tho.

More headaches
More pain.

I can't stop tho.

When will you stop then?
Never.

-MF

Fuck that

TBH
It makes me so mad seeing you with that nigga
My fucking blood starts boiling
That was supposed to be me
Now this nigga is gets so see all the things i showed you
I know i can't be selfish, you should be happy.
But fuck that.
I still want you
I still love you
Come back to me baby
I'm not scared to beg.
I still think about us
Please tell me you do too.

-MF

Not even slightly interested.

I'm on page 81.
Will people even make it this far?
What if they put the book down, a long time ago?
Who are you kidding,
You aren't a fucking poet.
You should just stop writing.
People aren't interesting in what you have to say.
No one gives a fuck about you.
No one ever has!
Why would you think this time would be different?
You should've stopped at page one.
Matter of fact, you made a mistake even writing down the title.
Just go back to whatever hole you tried escaping from.
No one is interested.

-MF

High and low sugar

There are so many high moments,
There are so many low moments.
The low ones are what scares me.
I don't know what to do

-MF

Drift Away

I invite you to drift away with me,
I've had enough of this town.
All we really need is each other anyway.
What do you say?

-MF

Boxes

Manny don't talk like that,
Manny don't dress like that.
Box
Box
Box
Stop trying to put me in it.
Have you ever sat back and thought,
I can be two different people at once?
I don't always want to sound like a book.
I don't always want to sound hood.
So I pick and chose.
And you judge me.
Let me live please.
I'm still trying to figure it out.

-MF

Hurtful Pleasure

My nose is bleeding,
I have to use the other nostril now.
God dam,
Thats some good shit.

-MF

Lost and found..

As a kid i was lost,
All i wanted was to be found.
But no one ever came.
All of a sudden, being alone didn't feel so bad.
I realized being lost means there's still a lot to be discovered.
I'm comfortable in the dark.
This is home for me.

-MF

ROBIN WILLIAMS

You can be successful and depressed at the same time
I feel this way everyday.
So many accolades.
But no one to talk to.
What do i keep chasing?
Better yet what do i keep running from?
I won't lie i've thought about ending it before.
The pressure feels so overwhelming at times.
This is how robin williams must've been feeling.
I've called the hotline but that didn't help.
Suicidal thoughts keep radiating.
A lot hides under this smile.

-MF

Scattered thoughts.

The pistol is in my hand,
My hands are wobbly.
I'm terrified.
I think today will be the day I actually go through with it.
I usually never have the balls to do it.
Who will miss me when I'm gone?
That doesn't matter anymore.

-Manny Flores

Disconnected

Disconnected from my friends
Disconnected from the classroom
Disconnected from the world
Can you imagine being 1/1 ?
No one understands me.
I'm constantly being told I should look like this.
I should look like that.
Things are very disconnected.

-MF

UCDavis

Why can't life be as simple as playing with bugs?
I think we all need to be like carly.
Simplistic yet loving.
We need to play with bugs and stop trippin.
Fuck all that high end shit.
Let's go research some bees.
Life is better when we worry less.
I need to take a trip to uc davis.

-MF

Masquerade Ball

The way we hide our pain is scary,
You wouldn't even know it.
Better yet you wouldn't even know what to do with it.
Mental scars,
Physical scars,
Abusive scars,
My body is covered in them.
Do you even know who I really am?
Of course you don't.
You think I'm this perfect person
But, if you only knew.

-MF

Mysterious girl

To Amanda: Every wound leaves a scar, but every scar tells a story.

A lot changed in my mind,
Mysterious girl.
All the things that make you, you.
Nothing will ever change that
Don't you know that i will be here?
Always.

-MF

Pain

We are strangers,
But what we have in common is pain.
Pain is universal
Pain makes us human
I hate that I suffered,
But I would never wish the pain away
Pain is exhausting
But pain taught me a valuable lesson
I'm a survivor.

-MF

Smile, Beautiful.

Even if the sky doesn't shine,
Smile.
Your happiness should not be predicated around anything temporary.
I love it when you smile.
The whole world lights up.
I think you're beautiful.
Gorgeous girl,
Keep smiling.
I love it.

-MF

Hella Sorry

I'm really sorry,
Im man enough to admit my mistakes.
I have done so many people shady in the past.
Mostly women.
I'm sorry.
Karma will catch up to me.
So don't worry about that,
I'll get mine eventually.
I've come to terms with it.

-MF

Dear Trump

I know you don't know me but im manny,
Im undocumented.
I also have degrees.
I'm getting my PhD in education
I can contribute to the country
But you want me to go back to mine
This is my country
Isn't it?
I like most things you like.
What do you say?
Let's be friends.

-MF

Future

I wish the future was here already
I'm tired
I'm tired of having to wake up at 6AM
I wish things were better
I know they will tho
It's almost 2018
This year has to be the one.
All my dreams will come true.

-MF